THERE IS A WAY

www.fast-print.net/store.php

There is a way

ISBN 978-178035-003-5

First published 2011 by
FASTPRINT PUBLISHING
Peterborough, England.

PAT PEACOCK

THERE IS A WAY

SPIRITUAL ANSWERS TO LIFE'S CHALLENGES

There is a Way

Also by Pat Peacock

Books:

My Search For Truth – paperback
How To Re-create Your Life – paperback
A Past Life – paperback

Booklets:

A Guide to the Development of Mediumship
An Introduction to Spiritualism

CD – covering first two books, booklets & Thoughts for every month of the Year – For reading on computer and/or printing

www.patpeacockspiritualism.com
telephone 01798 342897
3 Mulberry Court, Meadow Way,
Petworth, GU28 0EP

ACKNOWLEDGEMENTS

I would like to thank all those who have helped and encouraged me whilst writing this book whether they are on earth or in Spirit.

I know from experience that if you really want to live a happier and more fulfilling life and follow the methods in this book you too will find happiness and joy on your life's journey.

I dedicate this book to everyone who is seeking a better understanding of life and how to benefit from discovering their Spiritual Source.

May you all have success on your journey through your earthly life.

"I believe that the very purpose of our life is to seek happiness"

Dalai Lama

CONTENTS

INTRODUCTION

The intention of this book is to provide easy guidance for you to follow to enable you to live the best possible life. Your life is meant to be happy and joyful while you are experiencing the many colourful contrasts that you encounter on your earthly journey.

A great deal has been written about how to succeed in life both materially and spiritually. This book shows you how to use your spiritual nature in every area of your life. Many books have been written about the Law of Attraction including 'The Secret' by Rhonda Bryne. Some people have found that it works for them and others have been disappointed.

Since 'The Secret' was published there have been other books written, pointing out that this book has omitted important information which may be why some people have been disappointed when they found 'The Secret' didn't work for them.

There is a Way

If you want to read more about The Law of Attraction the best material is available from www.abraham-hicks.com

On this site you will find a great deal of information about Esther and Jerry Hicks and their work. There are CDs as well as books available and plenty of details of their work with Abraham. You can also subscribe to receiving a daily motivational quote.

The Law of Attraction does work but there are certain principles which need to be understood in order for you to *allow* it to work for you. This Law is working all the time for everyone but unknowingly you can prevent it from working to your advantage.

The guidelines in this book are not new and are in nearly all the ancient writings of every religion. Over the centuries man has made his own rules and creeds according to his religious beliefs. As a result of this, life has become more complicated. As man's knowledge has evolved, his understanding has not moved forward at the same pace.

This book has been kept as simple as possible so that it's readily understandable to all who want to live a life of happiness, joy and purpose.

By following these principles you can achieve great things. You have the power within yourself to do so – the message is here for you – the rest is up to you.

Approach this book with an open mind and consider every aspect on its own merits. Test the principles for yourself and see whether your life improves. It makes no difference where you are on your earthly journey the same principles apply.

The only decision you need to make is how you would like your life to be and then maintain as much as possible your connection with your Spiritual Source.

Some Philosophies use the terms Higher Self or Higher Consciousness to describe your Spiritual Source. It doesn't matter which term you use as they all refer to the same spiritual part of you.

If you have been drawn to this book, it's the right time for you to begin to realise that you are a *powerful creator* and have the ability to succeed in every area of your life.

I have deliberately repeated some things in this book because the principles are very important.

~ ~ ~ ~ ~ ~

" The strongest principle of growth lies in human choice"

George Eliot

THIS IS YOUR LIFE

This is your life - it's unique. No other person will have the same story or travel the same journey through life. This is your story and what you make of your journey is entirely up to you. No one else can take the journey for you, no one else may make your decisions or make you alter your direction. Your journey is in your own hands. Make of it what you will but ensure that it's a journey of fulfillment, happiness and joy.

Along the journey you'll receive many gifts to help you and many opportunities. You'll also encounter many problems to overcome. The journey is not always a straight road. It's a journey full of ups and downs, twists and turns and it's these events that add to the adventure. The contrasts and changes that you encounter in your life add interest and further opportunities.

You are living in an expanding Universe and you are expanding yourself during your journey. As you expand you are helping the Universe in its own expansion.

You have a choice – you always have a choice. You can either travel your journey in the spirit of adventure or you can allow life to pass you by without taking much notice and miss the joy and happiness of truly living – of being ALIVE!

At times in your life you may think that you have no choice. Everyone has that thought sometimes. Stop and think for a moment – you can choose whether you accept or reject anything, you can choose whether to act or not, you can choose whether to allow someone else to control you.

The most important choice of all is that of your thoughts. You may not be aware at this moment whether you are a positive or negative thinking person. Your thoughts are with you all the time and in a single day thousands of thoughts pass through your mind.

There is a Way

Some of the thoughts you allow to slip through, others you hold on to and reflect upon, others you push away and some, possibly only a few, you recognise as unwanted thoughts and you replace them with better, more hopeful and positive thoughts.The latter thoughts are the ones which will lead you to fulfil your purpose. You can train your mind to recognise more of these thoughts and use them to lighten your journey, make you more positive and make the journey more adventurous.

If you are uncertain whether you are a positive or negative thinking person there is a way to find out. Your emotions will tell you how you feel. If you are thinking *positive* thoughts you'll be feeling happy with your life. Negative thoughts will make you feel unhappy or discontented.

The cause of your unhappiness is not due to the problems in your life. It is due to your ATTITUDE towards those problems. Do you see them as *positive* challenges which will make your life better as you solve them? Or, do you see only negative problems that will drag you down and make your life worse? The journey of life is always beset with problems to solve and it's the difficulty experienced in finding solutions that cause the greatest anxiety in life.

Some of your problems have relatively easy solutions but others are far more difficult. The success of your journey and your happiness is dependant on how you face your problems. However far you've travelled, you will already have been faced with problems as this is a part of life.

If you want to live a life full of joy and happiness this book will help you find a way of solving your problems as and when they arise. If you allow a problem to remain unsolved it will lodge itself in the back of your mind and will keep rearing itself to remind you that this is something you should deal with. When you have several unsolved problems you'll find that your journey becomes one of confusion and anxiety.

There is a Way

Always live in the NOW with the intention of doing everything you want to and everything you can to complete your journey in fine style without limiting yourself and without having regrets. Learn to live your dreams now and don't put them to one side for the future. Too many people say 'one day I will do what I want to' and they never find the right time and then one day it's too late. There is a saying: 'don't die with your song unsung'. Sing it from your heart!

There is a purpose to everything that happens to you even though you may be unaware of this at the time. During your journey you'll meet many people, some who can help you and other people who turn to you for help.

People always come into your life for a purpose. They always appear at exactly the right time. Your soul intention is to meet and in the meeting each gives something to the other. It may be a few words of comfort, encouragement, support or a new idea. These people are like signposts on your journey.

You may meet a person only once but what you receive will have a lasting impact on your life and you may change your direction as a result. You may meet someone who walks beside you for a while as each has a great deal to share with the other. You may meet someone who remains with you until the end of your earthly life and together you each fulfil your life's purpose.

Consider for a moment the people who have already had an impact on your life. Ask yourself whether you would be where you are today if you hadn't met them.

Everything in your life has a purpose. You may be stimulated by a book, a film, a television programme, a wonderful holiday, something you decide to study or a previously unknown ability you suddenly discover that you have.

Remember: *This is your life journey and what you make of it is up to you.* If you look back on your journey so far you'll discover that there has been something linking the major events in your life.

Some people call this the 'golden chain' or 'golden ladder'. Without these events, you wouldn't be where you are today.

You are today, in this moment exactly where you should be. All the decisions or choices you've made in your life have brought you to this place. You could write the story of your life up to now and this will clarify the previous sentence. It does not have to be in book form – it can be in the form of notes. Remember it's your story and you don't have to show it to anyone.

You now have an opportunity to take a new look at your life and decide what aspects bring you joy and happiness and what aspects you need to work on.

Only you can do this if you want to be in control of your own life. When you consider this you'll probably find that a number of questions will come into your mind. Some of these questions you'll be able to answer immediately and others may not be so easy.

There is a Way

You may find that you're standing at crossroads and have to choose which way to go next. You may find that you're going in the right direction and are ready to take a step forward. You may find that you need to change direction. By the time you finish reading this book I hope you'll have found an answer that will lead you forward.

~ ~ ~ ~ ~ ~

"It takes's courage to face our own shortcomings, and wisdom to do something about it."

Edgar Cayce

PART I

INTRODUCING A NEW WAY TO LIVE

"If the mind is happy, not only the body but the whole world will be happy. So one must find out how to become happy oneself. Wanting to reform the world without discovering one's true self is like trying to cover the whole world with leather to avoid the pain of walking on stones and thorns. It is much simpler to wear shoes".

Ramana Maharshi

WHO AM I?

You are a Spiritual Being temporarily inhabiting a physical body. When you were born on earth you brought with you a portion of your spiritual being and the rest of your being remained in the unseen World of Spirit.

When you arrived on earth it was your intention to remain connected to the portion of your Being in the unseen world to help you to live a successful, happy and joyful life. It's this part of you that is pure source energy and holds all the answers to the many questions that you have about life, its purpose and how to live in harmony with The Source of all.

This Source is what you may call God, the Creator, the Divine Spirit or the Divine Source from where you have inherited eternal life. Your present earthly journey is only a very small part of your eternal life and when it has ended you will return to your Spiritual Source which is always connected to the Divine Source.

You have lived many lives and the wisdom and understanding you have gained from these lives is all contained in your unseen Spiritual Source.

The Divine Source is pure energy and that part of yourself that is in the Spirit World is pure energy. All life, not just human life is energy and vibration. The vibration of earth is slower than that of the Spirit World and therefore slower than your Spiritual Source or your higher consciousness.

When you took on human form you were born into a family, in a part of the world or race that already had a belief system and during your childhood years you were taught the beliefs of your family unit.You also learned from your education and from your peers. The society in which you belonged will have had a strong influence on the early part of your earthly journey and may still be controlling your adult life.

You may or may not be aware of the effect that these early influences are having on your life. As you read further you'll start to discover some beliefs that you may now want to change. They may be beliefs which served you in the past but as you have grown in your understanding of the purpose of your life it's often necessary to let go of some of your earlier beliefs.

Whatever your upbringing, you are still a spiritual being and have access to your unseen Spiritual Source. As always you have the choice whether to access this or not. There are many people who don't understand that they are spiritual beings as well as those who do know that they are spiritual beings and either don't know how to access their source or don't wish to have this understanding.

~ ~ ~ ~ ~ ~

YOUR RESPONSIBITY

Much has been written about our responsibilities in life. *The most important responsibility you have is to maintain your connection with your Spiritual Source.*

There is a Way

When you are connected your journey becomes more joyful and harmonious. It isn't possible to remain connected all the time. It is possible to learn how to reconnect quickly and easily whenever you experience your disconnection.

If you are feeling good about your life you are connected. When you feel upset with your life you are disconnected.

When you're connected to your Spiritual Source, your physical and spiritual beings are vibrating at the same rate. When you are disconnected your physical being is vibrating at a lower rate than your Spiritual Source.

It's your responsibility to maintain the vibration of the physical part of you so that you are able to enjoy being connected to your Spiritual Source – to your Spiritual Self.

You can only make this connection for yourself through your emotional guidance.

~ ~ ~ ~ ~ ~

YOUR EMOTIONAL GUIDANCE

In order to find your emotional guidance you have to *allow* yourself to connect to your Spiritual Source. First of all you have to let go of any resistance you may be feeling and *allow* yourself to make your connection.

The easiest way to do this is to practise being aware of your breathing. Control your breath by breathing in and out slowly and deeply. As you inhale allow yourself to breath in the vibration of Spirit. As you exhale *allow* yourself to let go of any negative thoughts of resistance. As you continue to practise this for about ten to fifteen minutes you will gradually begin to feel more relaxed and your thoughts will turn away from any worries you are experiencing in your life.

This will then *allow* you to focus on feeling good and the knowledge that your life's journey is going to be much happier and more joyous than ever before.

There is a Way

Your aim is to feel good whatever is happening in your outside world. This is your inner world which feels good and will lead to happiness.

How you are feeling at any moment will always tell you whether you are connected to your Spiritual Source. This is the most important achievement you can make as you'll never again have to worry about any difficulties in your life because you will have the ultimate way of solving and overcoming them.

When you decided to incarnate you were looking forward to being a *creator* and as you created so you expanded yourself along with the people you met on your journey.

The problems you experience on your journey cause you to create and expand as you find your solutions.

Your Spiritual Source is always aware of the problems you are experiencing and has the solutions ready for you. This is why connecting to your Source is so important.

There is a Way

Without having problems you wouldn't have the opportunity to create and expand. As you expand yourself you also become involved in the expansion of the whole. Thus everyone benefits not just you.

As you begin to understand this, you'll discover your life's purpose and your journey will be far happier and exciting as a result.

Before trying to solve specific problems find time to become more aware of being connected to your Spiritual Source. Once you have achieved this and really know what it feels like, it will be much easier to use this to solve your difficulties.

Every time you solve a problem you have made a decision and, as you let go of any resistance to your past, you'll be creating and expanding. This gives your journey excitement - a real sense of achievement. Always remember that you are living in an expanding Universe and *your* creating and expanding will affect the whole of creation.

There is a Way

You are an individual and only you can find the right way for you to relax, control your breathing and make your connection to your Spiritual Source. Once you've found your ideal way you can use it every time you discover that you have become disconnected. When you are separated from your Spiritual Source, the problems and your journey become more difficult until reconnect.

It doesn't matter which method you use to connect – one way will be right for you. Always choose the one which is easiest for you. The process is not difficult, its actually very simple.

Be patient with yourself. Don't try to hurry through this section. If you ignore this section you'll find that you have to return to it later as your problem solving will be more difficult without mastering this step first.

~ ~ ~ ~ ~ ~

THE LAW OF ATTRACTION

There are Universal Laws which hold the Universe together including the Law of Gravity. We don't think about this very often, it just is. If the Law of Gravity failed everything would spin out of orbit and the result would be chaos. Although we appear to be standing still the earth is rotating all the time at a very fast rate but we take this for granted and don't think about it.

Our furniture appears to be solid but the scientists tell us that it is mainly empty space with particles vibrating at a specific frequency which holds it together.

Understanding the Law of Attraction is vital to the expansion of your life. This Law is always working in every area of life. It works for everyone all the time whether you understand it or not.

LIKE ALWAYS ATTRACTS LIKE

In other words, you are attracting into your life, every day, whatever you are focusing your thoughts on. This Law operates whether your thoughts are positive or negative. If your thoughts are positive you attract what you want. If your thoughts are negative you attract what you don't want.

You may be attracting what you don't want because you don't know what you do want. This can apply to any area of life.

This is why it's so important to decide what you want so that you can focus your thoughts in the right direction.

Resistance is the only thing that prevents what we desire from coming to us. Focusing positive thoughts in the direction of those things we really want begins the slow release of resistance. It's like clearing away an unwanted dam so the river can flow and when it does, the fresh water brings to us our desires.

~ ~ ~ ~ ~ ~

PROBLEMS

We all experience problems on our life journey and these problems should be looked at as challenges. They always fall within three specific categories:

RELATIONSHIPS
FINANCIAL
HEALTH AND WELLBEING

If you can learn to use the Law of Attraction and know how to connect to your Spiritual Source then every challenge you may encounter can be solved. There is a Spiritual solution to every problem and the answer is to be found within your Spiritual Source.

In one way or another all the challenges you encounter on your journey you have attracted. You may have attracted these deliberately or been unaware that you are attracting what you don't want.

One of the reasons for doing this is that we cannot decide what we do want. We find it difficult to choose between one direction and another.

Think of your journey through life as though it is a journey from London to Glasgow. Before you set out you know where you are going. What you have to decide is the route you're going to take. There are several different routes you could take from London to Glasgow and in the same way there are different routes you can take on your life journey.

There is one certainty on your life journey and that is that having taken on an earthly, physical body, at some time in the future you will no longer need it as you will be returning to Spirit.

How you make the journey of your life is your choice and responsibility and nobody but you can decide which route you're going to take.This is why it's so important to decide what kind of journey you want to create.

Initially, your journey will have been conditioned by those around you and you may have experienced problems if you didn't conform to their opinions.

As you reach adulthood you have more say in what you decide to believe as you travel. It's true that what you think are your beliefs and, if you've been taught that you cannot do something, you may carry that belief with you throughout your entire life.

As a child you may have been told you were stupid and this is something that is difficult to overcome. You may have suffered poor health as a child and always thought of yourself as being prone to illness and this, also, can be a difficult challenge.

If someone suddenly told you that you could do anything you wanted, have everything you wanted, live the life you wanted, and be the person you wanted, would you be able to believe them? At first it would seem that you were being told a fairy story and that it couldn't possibly be true. You would more than likely deny the possibility and say that others may be able to but not you.

We grow up with a fixed idea in our minds about what we are capable of doing or achieving without having tried to do something different.

Often children are told that they have been born poor and will always be poor and there is nothing they can do about it. That is their lot in life. Rubbish! What about the people who started their lives in very poor circumstances and made up their minds that they would succeed and prove that anyone could do what they wanted if they put their minds to living differently.

Think about the people who, against all odds, have overcome physical conditions. Think about the people who, even as children, had a burning desire to achieve something their parents at the time said was impossible and yet have gone on to achieve their dream.

It's good to have a dream, to be passionate about it, to believe it's possible and to achieve it. You can enjoy your dream and your journey, find happiness in your fulfilment and realise your purpose in life.

Your dream may be a small dream, a very large dream or any size inbetween. The size of your dream doesn't matter it's your belief that you can achieve it that's important.The responsibility for achieving it is yours – you own the dream – it's yours to achieve.

Pause for a moment and ask yourself the following questions:

- *Do you know what you really want for your journey?*
- *What do you think about most of the time?*

When you're passionate about something you'll realise that this is what occupies most of your thoughts. You may wake up in the morning with the thought immediately in your mind. You may find yourself thinking about it when you should be thinking about something else.

On the other hand you may find that most of your waking thoughts are of worry about the problems in your life. These may fall into any of the three categories mentioned earlier. You may have a problem within each of the three categories.

- *Have you ever thought that a relationship problem, a financial problem and a health problem could all be solved using the same method?*

- *Have you ever thought that constantly worrying about your problems could be causing the problems to grow worse?*

- *Have you ever thought that worry itself could be causing your problems?*

Let's take a closer look at the three categories:

RELATIONSHIPS

If your problem is concerning a relationship, have you asked yourself:

- *Why has this problem occurred?*
- *Am I expecting the other person to conform to my beliefs?*
- *Am I expecting the other person to be perfect?*
- *Am I expecting too much from that other person?*
- *Am I giving enough or too much of myself?*
- *Havc I taken on a responsibility that doesn't belong to me?*

You cannot expect anyone to change unless they want to change.

The only person you can change is yourself. In many instances the problems in relationships are caused because each person thinks they know best how the other person should be and as long as this belief exists so will the problem.

Another reason for relationship problems is thinking you are right in every situation. Nobody is right all the time. Sometimes one person is right and sometimes the other. If you think you are right, and are always determined to be right, you'll find that you have very stormy relationships and life journey.

Ask yourself:

- *Do I enjoy a stormy journey?*
- *Would I like my life to be happier and more joyful?*

Relationship problems include your family, your friends, people you work with and people you meet at the clubs, societies and churches to which you belong.These problems often cause a great deal of unhappiness, anger, bitterness and distress not only to the people directly concerned but also to others.

Relationship problems often lead to health problems. They may also cause financial worries. The result, instead of having one problem to worry about you have three or more problems to solve all stemming from the same source.

~ ~ ~ ~ ~ ~

FINANCIAL

- *Do you believe that you live in a world of limited resources?*
- *Do you believe that you don't deserve to have something you want?*
- *Do you believe that only privileged people can have what they want?*
- *Do you believe, because you have been told in the past that you are poor, that you will always have to be poor?*

Imagine, one day someone told you that you could have anything you wanted. What if you were told that you lived in an Abundant Universe where there is enough for everyone.

Would you believe it or would you still believe that you didn't deserve it and that you were not included? Perhaps you would respond by saying that if you were rich you wouldn't be able to handle it or wouldn't know what to do with it.

Imagine for a moment that you won millions in a lottery. Would you then begin to worry about how to deal with it, how it would affect your lifestyle, your friendships and possibly your health? If you think that would happen then you would just be exchanging one set of worries for another.

In one way your life would be easier and in another it would become more difficult or more complicated.

Your financial worries can be upsetting your relationships and your health.

~ ~ ~ ~ ~ ~

HEALTH AND WELLBEING

Most people want to be healthy as good health makes your life's journey far more pleasant. There are a few people who use illness as a way of obtaining constant attention from people but these are a minority. If you have a health problem, either minor or serious, do you:

- *Constantly think about your illness?*
- *Relate your health problems to all who will listen?*
- *Worry about whether the health problem will get worse and what will happen if it does?*
- *Say to yourself, "Why me? It's not fair"?*

The cause of your health problem may be due to a number of factors. For example, do you:

- *Think that because your relatives died from a certain illness you will obviously do the same?*
- *Think that when there is a flu epidemic you will also catch it?*
- *Think that a small pain somewhere in your body is definitely due to a serious illness?*

There is a Way

Worrying constantly about your state of ill health attracts more ill health.

We are conditioned to believe our health must deteriorate as we become older. Do you think that this is inevitable? It isn't. It's your *ATTITUDE* to ageing that decides.

Your life's journey can and should be enjoyable at every stage. If you find you're thinking the best part of your life is over and you are too old to enjoy yourself or find something new to interest you, then this is how you will spend the last years of your life. You can decide which way you want to spend your remaining years.

It's important to be aware that your *ATTITUDE* towards health problems can also affect relationship and financial problems.

~ ~ ~ ~ ~ ~

YOUR JOURNEY IS YOUR CHOICE

You should be in control of your life.

How do you want your life to be?

Ask yourself this question. You may have an answer immediately or you may not know exactly what you want.

If you were asked what you disliked about your present life how many things would you list? Most people spend a great deal of their life complaining and thinking about what they don't want and less time talking about what is good about their life. Ask yourself whether you do this and watch yourself over the next few days to see which way you are thinking.

Begin to ask yourself how you are feeling.

- *Am I feeling happy or miserable?*
- *Does it feel better when I am feeling happy or when I am feeling miserable?*

- *How do I really want to feel?*

Much has been written about the power of positive versus negative thought. If you're not aware of your thoughts you'll not be aware of how often you are thinking positively and how often negatively. A quick and easy way of discovering the answer to this is to stop and ask yourself – "***how do I feel***"?

If you're feeling happy and joyful and good about your life then you are well on your way to being a positive thinking person. If you're feeling worried, miserable, anxious or upset then at that time you're being a negative thinking person. Most people fluctuate between the two.

When you're feeling good about your life you are connected to your Spiritual Source and when you're feeling bad you are disconnected.

In Part III of this book you'll find information on how to connect to your Spiritual Source, often referred to as

There is a Way

'Higher Consciousness', how to discover that you have become disconnected and how to reconnect quickly and easily.

~ ~ ~ ~ ~ ~

WHERE TO START

There is only one place that you can start and that is exactly where you are.

It isn't possible to begin in the past that you have already lived and if you plan to start next week, next month, at the beginning of a new year, the chances are that you will never make the necessary changes.

God, the Divine Source, is also the Creator. You have originated from that Divine Source and are also a *creator*. The spiritual part of you that is living your earthly journey is a *creator* and your Spiritual Source flows through you.

Since you incarnated on the earth you have been creating your life's journey. You have created all the circumstances in your life. You have attracted this book you are reading.

I can hear some of you saying to yourself:

- *'How can I possibly have created my life with the problems I have?*
- *Surely if I was a creator I would have created something far better?*
- *I don't like what I have created.*
- *How can I possibly be responsible for the life I have created?*
- *Some of the responsibility for my problems must lie with society, the Government, my family or my partner.*

Try to keep an open mind at this point and know that it's the beliefs and thoughts that you have carried with you that have caused you to create where you are today.

Remember that this is not the end of your journey and it isn't how your journey has to be. You are a *creator* always and as such you can begin to create a better journey for yourself. *You can begin this right now.* You don't have to ask for permission to do this, it's your choice. If you choose what feels good to you then you'll be on your way to a far better journey.

~ ~ ~ ~ ~ ~

THE FIRST STEP

CHOOSE HOW YOU LIVE YOUR JOURNEY

Give yourself permission to look at where you are at this moment and decide what you would like to improve in your life. Don't think about how you're going to do it – just focus on how you would like your life to be at some time in the future. Don't set a target date or listen to any thought that may come into your mind telling you that what you want is impossible.

For the first time in your life, believe that absolutely everything you can think or dream of is possible. ***IT IS!***

To make it easier for yourself either find something in your life at the moment you can feel happy or joyful about, or think of a particular memory when you felt happy, or listen to some music that makes you feel better, or go for a walk, look at a beautiful picture that inspires you or a beautiful flower.

As you do this you'll find yourself thinking more positively and becoming calmer.

Another way is to find a quiet place where you won't be disturbed and sit and focus on your breathing for about 10 minutes. If you find your focus moving to your present problems gently bring your focus back to your breathing. You cannot be focusing on your breathing and your problems at the same time.

If you find it easy to meditate, after a while, focus your thought on a beautiful scene in your mind. Do this before you carry out the following task. It will make it easier.

Remember that your Spiritual Source knows what you want. By doing the above exercise first you will be connecting to the 'Source' you.

Write down how you want your life to be. Remember you can always add to it later or change something. I would suggest that you give it a title. Here are a few suggestions for titles but if you prefer choose one of your own. It's important to choose a title that feels right to you:

My Unfolding Life
How I want my Life to be
What I want to attract

The most important thing is to set an *intention.* Don't worry if you think that you haven't thought of enough changes that you want to make or you have one change that is particularly urgent. You'll find that, as you begin changing your ideas on what is most important, your life will change.

This is part of moving forward into a more exciting and exhilarating journey.

The important key is what you INTEND AND HOW YOU FEEL as this is always the result of how you are THINKING. You'll find yourself asking the question, "how do I feel?" and this is good. It will help you to know yourself better and understand why you allow certain things to happen and why you've attracted them in the past.

With this knowledge you'll learn how to avoid attracting unwanted people and things into your life in the future.

~ ~ ~ ~ ~ ~

"I care what I feel. I intend to feel good"
Anon

.

PART II

THE LAW OF ATTRACTION

You have the power to attract and create whatever you want

"By paying attention to the way you feel and then choosing thoughts that feel the very best, you are managing your own vibration which means you are controlling your own point of attraction – which means you are creating your own reality."

'Abraham'

THE LAW OF ATTRACTION

The Law of Attraction works for everyone – there are no exceptions. Like attracts like. Whatever you are focusing on you'll attract. If you keep your thoughts and conversations on what is wrong or missing from your life you will attract more of what is wrong and missing from your life. This is the mistake most people make.

The other mistake is being dissatisfied with your life and at the same time not knowing how you really want your life to be. Unless you know what you want you can't put your mind towards obtaining it.

If you haven't decided yet what you really want, pause, and decide now!

You live in an abundant Universe and there is plenty for everyone. Because one person takes from the Universe, it doesn't mean that there is less for anyone else.

You have the power to attract to you everything you desire. You are a *creator*.

You are the *creator* of your physical life and are responsible for what you create.

Babies and small children are still connected to their non-physical part and become disconnected by the influences around them. If they are born into families who have no understanding of their child's spirituality, they will be taught to use only their physical senses and gradually their connection to their Source will weaken.

The secret is to remain connected to the non-physical part of you as much as possible and encourage children to do the same.

The Law of Attraction needs to be fully understood before you learn ways of maintaining your connection with your Spiritual Source.

When you begin to work with the Law of Attraction you can expect many changes to occur in your life. If you are afraid of changes, and have doubts that you will be able to cope with the changes, then you'll experience difficulty with the new life you are creating.

You have to be *positive* that this new way of living will be exciting. You'll make wonderful discoveries and meet like-minded people. You'll also be able to stop worrying about the problems of your life as now you have a way of solving them.

It's important, once you've decided what you want, that you believe it's possible to achieve it without knowing how you can achieve it. All you need to know is that you can achieve it. In other words, believe you deserve it, release any doubt and allow it to come to you.

Once you have identified the problem, stop thinking about it as a problem. Consider it as a challenge and focus on the solution.You already know that you can't change anyone else. You are focusing on changing yourself, your view of a situation, your attitude towards it and finding an answer which will bring you peace of mind, happiness, enjoyment and improve your journey.

Realise that as your journey improves you will become a happier person and your happiness will affect everyone you meet. You may not always be aware of how you have affected other people, or how many, but we all do.

You are working towards a happier journey for yourself. You may think that this is being selfish but if you become a happier person you will have more to give to others.

~ ~ ~ ~ ~ ~

LAW OF ATTRACTION IN RELATIONSHIPS

During your lifetime you'll have experienced challenges with relationships. These may have been with parents, husband/wife, children, friends, work colleagues, neighbours, the list can be endless.

These challenges can be carried with you as a burden that you have difficulty in releasing. These burdens may be in your past or in your present and until they are released they prevent you from living a really enjoyable life. They are always nagging away in the background and they keep resurfacing to destroy your peace of mind.

The more you think about these challenges the more of the same type you attract. These are things you don't want to attract and the only way to stop attracting what you don't want is to begin to attract what you do want. In order to achieve this it's necessary to *release* the unwanted situations you have attracted. By connecting with your Spiritual Source a solution can be found.

This doesn't mean that you have to condone the actions of others. It means that you have to *allow* others to be themselves and live according to their beliefs whilst you hold onto your beliefs.

Thoughts of resentment, jealousy, anger, injustice and judgement hurt the person who is thinking them more than the person to whom the thoughts are being directed. This can have a serious effect on your health and future relationships.

Striving always to be right is also detrimental as nobody is always right. If you are having a challenge with someone who thinks they are always right and in opposition to what you think is right, one way is to say calmly – “you may be right, I hadn’t thought of it in that way. I’ll think about it”. This will prevent a confrontation and you’ll feel much better than if you had caused an argument.

Appreciating the good qualities in a person rather than highlighting their faults is a way of creating a better relationship between you and the other person. This is particularly important when relating to children.

Children thrive on praise and suffer greatly on criticism.They won’t always do what you want or expect of them.

They are learning and don't always get it right. Adults also are learning and don't always get it right. There are occasions where the child is right and the parent is wrong.

Another mistake that is made with relationship challenges is that too much time is spent in relating them to anyone who will listen. The more they are related, the more of the same situations you'll attract and the heavier the burden becomes. The more thoughts are given to the burden, the less chance there is of finding a solution.

Some of the relationship challenges start in a very trivial way and over the course of time the real cause can be forgotten. Usually trivial things can be dealt with quickly and easily if the solution is found straight away and the challenge is not allowed to fester and grow.

Difficulties with your relationships can lead to both financial and health issues. If you solve your relationship challenges your financial situation and health will start to improve.

~ ~ ~ ~ ~ ~

THE LAW OF ATTRACTION IN FINANCE

There are many reasons for financial challenges, such as –

- *not having enough money,*
- *being in debt,*
- *worrying about the increasing cost of living,*
- *being unable to earn enough to support your family,*
- *worrying about losing your job and income,*
- *not being able to find a job to support your family or yourself.*

You may have been brought up in a family where money was always short and often heard the phrase, 'money doesn't grow on trees'. You may have been brought up with the belief that some people are poor and will remain so whilst others are very rich.

Your expectation may be that you'll always have to struggle to have enough money for the necessities and there will never be any money for the luxuries that some people appear to enjoy.

If this is your belief you have to look at this belief and begin to let go of it. Your belief of lack is causing more lack to come into your life. Remember your thoughts always become your reality.

Begin to believe that you live in an *abundant Universe* where there is plenty for everyone and that includes you. As soon as you change your belief your finances will begin to improve.

Whatever the cause of any present financial worries, let go of them, know that you deserve to receive and allow yourself to receive the money which is ready to flow to you.

Remember you are a *creator* and have the power to change your circumstances, financial or otherwise. Always focus on improving your financial situation rather than focusing on your lack of money or debts. All the time you focus on lack this is what you'll attract.

You may have been brought up in the belief that it's not spiritual to have money because money is evil. This is not so.

Money is energy and is exchanged for goods and for personal growth. As you buy something you are allowing the creator of the product to earn their money and, as the exchange takes place, you are growing.

Think of it like this. Whatever product you buy, there are numerous people involved in producing it, from the creator, the manufacturer of the product, the manufacturers of all the components, through to the person who sells it to you. Every person in this chain is earning money because you decided to buy the product. You are involved in a chain of people who have provided what you want to purchase and everyone in that chain has benefited by your decision to buy.

Worries of a financial nature always have an adverse effect on your relationships and your health. A large number of health challenges are the result of worry and financial worries are top of the list.

~ ~ ~ ~ ~ ~

THE LAW OF ATTRACTION IN HEALTH

A healthy person has an advantage over a person who is sick. If you are healthy you have more energy and therefore are able to cope much better with the ups and downs in your life.

If you are enjoying good health you have more opportunities in the choices you make. You have fewer restrictions during your journey and as a consequence you have a more enjoyable life.

As soon as you become ill your energy becomes depleted. You cannot stop it happening. If you're ill and start to worry about your illness you deplete your energy even more. Worry uses up the energy with which you want to heal yourself of the illness. It becomes a vicious circle.

During our lifetime we all have some form of illness, either minor or major and it's how we choose to view our illness that dictates the speed of our recovery. Many of the minor illnesses could be avoided if we put the Law of Attraction into working for us rather than against us.

Do you say as winter approaches –

- *I always catch everything that is going round during the winter.*
- *I always suffer with colds, sore throats, flu and a bad cough during the winter.*
- *If I go into a room where someone is coughing and sneezing I know that I'll catch it'.*

People who think like that are attracting the illnesses. They expect to be ill and so they are. They don't want to be ill but they've convinced themselves that they will be ill as they always are, every winter. These are the types of illnesses that we attract because we are low in energy due to the worries we have in other areas of our lives.

You can also attract certain kinds of illnesses because you've been told that other members of the family suffered from a particular illness and died from it. Although you may not be aware of it, in the back of your mind you are expecting to get the same illness, and possibly die from it.

There may be a history in your family of people dying early, say in their fifties or sixties, and you may be anticipating that you won't live to old age.

The more you focus your thoughts on illness, talk about feeling ill, think that every minor ache or pain must be a very serious illness the more likely you are to become ill.

Your body has an immune system which is ready at all times to fight any illness you may have. Many people take so many different medications that their own immune system is unable to cope.

I'm not suggesting for one moment that there isn't value in modern medicines, nor am I suggesting that they should not be taken but to realise that your own immune system is capable of doing far more than most people think.

Many people are now interested in alternative forms of healing and a positive attitude towards the outcome is always beneficial.

Spiritual Healing works on healing the spirit and the cause of the illness rather than the disease itself. If you connect with your Spiritual Source, which is never sick, then healing of your Spirit which is at present living a physical earthly life, is guaranteed. As a result your physical body will produce its own healing because your lack of resistance *allows* the cells of your body to do what they do best – to be well.

Remember the more you think and talk about what is wrong the more of the same you will attract. The more you think of yourself as being purely a physical being the less connection you'll have with your Spiritual Source and this will reduce the ability for physical healing to take place.

When asking for healing for yourself or for another you should always be asking for what is for the Highest Good. Remember, that this physical life is temporary and it isn't for you to decide when it's the right time for anyone to return to Spirit. The Soul knows when it has chosen to go and you'll have a far better understanding of this concept when connected to your source.

Use the Law of Attraction to improve your health. Think about being well, think about building up your energy and using your connection to your Spiritual Source to achieve this.

There is a Way

Try not to live in your present illness. Instead, live in the *feeling* of what you *want.* Acceptance of your present health with an offering of compassion towards yourself is the first step on your journey towards reclaiming your health – your natural state of wellbeing.

If a friend of yours was ill, you would do anything to help them. Your heart would leap into action! Let that same heart leap for yourself, with the same compassion, the same love, the same acceptance and a willingness to know, beyond any shadow of doubt that '*There is a way*'.

~ ~ ~ ~ ~ ~

"My intention is to live my life enjoying perfect health".

Anon

PART III

CONNECTING TO YOUR SPIRITUAL SOURCE

"It is not your job to transform the world for others but it is your job to transform it for you. A state of appreciation is pure Connection to Source where there is no perception of lack."

'Abraham'

CONNECTING TO YOUR SPIRITUAL SOURCE

Do you know whether you are connected? What are the indications which tell you immediately that you are connected? Is it easy to discover the answer?

These are the questions that you may have been asking as you have read this book.

When you are feeling happy, joyful, at peace with yourself and your life you are connected.

When you are feeling unhappy, depressed, sad, miserable, fed up with your life you are disconnected.

You may be thinking to yourself – 'sometimes I must be connected and at other times disconnected'. This is true.

Nobody remains connected all the time but you can reach a point where you are connected most of the time. This is your goal, to be connected as often as possible, to recognise when you are disconnected and be able to reconnect as quickly as possible.

Your Spiritual Source always thinks the best about every situation in your physical life. It always thinks the best about your challenges. When you're thinking in the same postive way, you are working with your Spiritual Source. You are connected.

It's when this alignment occurs that you can find the best solutions to whatever is troubling you. If you are thinking negative thoughts you are out of alignment and have become disconnected and the solutions you are searching for are out of reach.

~ ~ ~ ~ ~ ~

HOW TO CONNECT

Your Spiritual Source, which is the non-physical part of you is vibrating at a higher frequency than your physical being. In order to connect to it, you have to find a way of raising your physical vibration.

Imagine you are feeling a bit down and a friends walks through your door with a big smile on her face holding two Danish pastries! You would instantly feel better. THAT is your physical vibration rising to a higher frequency. This is what emotion is - it's our guidance system. We can all feel our emotions. We can recognise when our frequency is low and take deliberate steps to raise it. When we feel better our vibration is higher and from that better feeling place, we can attract better things.

To benefit from the Law of Attraction and only attract what you really want, you have to lift your vibration to come into alignment with your non-physical counterpart.

You have to find something that will make you start to feel better. The best way to begin is by appreciating what you have now. Realise how much you have – not just material possessions – the people in your life that mean so much, your abilities, the wonders of nature, music, art, everything that uplifts you and makes you feel good.

Write down all the things that you have at the present time. It helps to make a list so you can refer back to it quickly at a time when you are feeling less good and obtain a very quick lift up.

There are several ways in which you can connect with your Spiritual Source.

One way is to sit quietly where you won't be disturbed. Close your eyes and go through the alphabet choosing a positive, happy word for each letter. For example, A for appreciation, B for beauty, C for carefree etc. As you think of each word, really feel the meaning of the word, as though you are drawing the essence of that word into your very being.

When you have finished going through the alphabet, try to remain in that feeling of positive happiness. If your thoughts drift to a situation that you are worrying about gently push it away and return to the feeling of happiness.

Another way is to sit quietly and listen to music. It doesn't matter what music you choose so long as you find it happy and uplifting.

Take a walk in the country or a park or sit in your garden. Feel the beauty of nature, listen to the birds, feel the wind on your face, look at the sky, watch the clouds and know that you are one with everything that is.

Stand on the shore looking out to sea, listen to the sound of the sea, the call of the seagulls, feel the sea spray on your face, touch the sand or pebbles and know that at that moment you are standing in the right place, that you belong.

Stand and look up at a clear night sky. Look at the moon and the stars, try to imagine how far away from you they are and realise that although you are able to see so many stars there is so much more that is beyond your vision.

Put a single flower into a vase and really examine it. Touch it, feel the petals, the leaves, the stem and notice the difference of feeling that you get as you touch the different parts. See if there is a perfume. Look into the centre of the flower, the shape, the number of petals. You'll most likely discover that, although you've seen this variety of flower before, you have not noticed how really beautiful it is.

Sit quietly in the dark and light a single candle. Enjoy the subdued lighting, watch the flickering of the flame, look into and see different colours within the flame, feel its warmth and see how it makes the room look and feel different. Take comfort from the candle and use it as a symbol of spiritual light.

You can think of other ways in which you are able to feel positive joy and pleasure. The above are merely suggested tools that you can use. While you are really immersed in the pleasure of your chosen method, you'll find that you're totally focused on something that makes you feel good and there's no room for negative thought at the same time.

It's like passing through a portal, a doorway, a gateway into a new and exciting experience. You've been through this doorway many times in your life when you've had moments of pure joy and happiness without realising that you have been connected to your Spiritual Source. These moments may have lasted a very short while or for longer periods depending on the reason for your joy.

You now know that you can have this experience at any time you wish. You know the secret of how to pass through this doorway and experience your connection. You also know how you feel when you are connected. You have aligned the physical part of you with the non-physical part of you.

You'll also know when you are not connected as you will have a completely different feeling. Your emotions will be different and you may experience anger, frustration, annoyance, distress and all the other emotions that come from the challenges of your life's journey.

You'll start to feel more strongly the contrast between when you are connected and when you are not. You'll become more aware of the *cause* of your disconnection.

The more you practise connecting with your Spiritual Source the easier it will become and the quicker you'll be able to reconnect.

Once you have achieved your connection you'll be able to use your creative power to create anything and everything you want in your life.

Part IV will show you ways of using your creative power to solve the problems in your life.

~ ~ ~ ~ ~ ~

CONNECTING TO OTHER SPIRITUAL SOURCES

While you're connected to your Spiritual Source you'll probably find that sometimes you become connected to a different Spiritual Being. This may be because the solution you are seeking can be solved better or quicker by another Spiritual Being. Just as on the earth plane, those in Spirit have different experiences and different skills and want to help you.

You may feel warmth as someone is drawing close to you and you should feel comfortable with this. As they draw close you may find that words come flooding into your mind and if this happens you should write them down. If the words come too quickly you should mentally ask them to slow down. The first time this happens if you can't record every word make notes.

Sometimes advice will be given as to where you should go or who you should contact on the earth to get the help you need. At other times the advice will be something that you can deal with yourself.

If you read about the lives of great inventors, composers, writers and artists, you'll find that many of them talk of being 'inspired' in their work by unknown Guides or Helpers. They say that they usually appear when the help is most needed. These Guides and Helpers are available for everyone and that includes you.

Sometimes they will tell you who they are but at other times they don't. It doesn't matter whether they give you a name or not it's the help they give which is important.

The more you become connected to your Spiritual Source the greater the help you can obtain from these unseen Spiritual Beings. They can become as much a part of your life's journey as your own Spiritual Source.

They can be especially helpful if you're wanting help of a specialist nature. If you believe they are available for you to call on, they will always answer your call.

You have a Guide who came with you when you incarnated onto the earth and remains with you throughout your life's journey. Your Guide is available at all times to offer you help and encouragement and when you're connected to your Spiritual Source you'll discover how much easier it is to receive communication from your Guide.

Your Guide cannot make decisions and live your life for you nor tell you what you must or must not do. Your Guide can only give you words of wisdom and answer your questions *if you ask.*

Always remember that the reason we don't receive the answers is often because we haven't asked the question.

ASK AND YOU'LL RECEIVE

Be positive in your asking and eagerly anticipate receiving your answer. Know that your answer may come in a variety of ways, not always in the way you are expecting.

You may find that you are directed to a book or magazine or you may meet someone and during a conversation with them, they will suddenly begin to talk about the subject you have been questioning.

You do not meet people by accident – they always have something to offer you or you have something that they need.

Once you learn to live your life and expect good things to happen to you, you'll understand the difference between living and existing. When you're really experiencing the fullness of life you'll find it far more exciting and every day will bring fresh surprises.

~ ~ ~ ~ ~ ~

PART IV

HOW TO USE YOUR CREATIVE POWER TO FIND SOLUTIONS TO YOUR CHALLENGES

"Our challenge, which is also a tremendous opportunity, is to open up to a literally life-changing way of thinking ourselves into existence."

Daniel Pinchbeck

Whatever your present difficulties, as you connect to your Spiritual Source, you have to leave these problems or challenges behind as they belong to your physical world. If you focus on them you will immediately become disconnected.

Your Spiritual Source only has solutions and if, in your mind, you state the challenges to which you are seeking a solution prior to making the connection the answers will be available to you.

Remember that your Spiritual Source is the pure part of you that is never affected by any challenges of the earthly world. Your Spiritual Source is always directly linked to the Divine Source and therefore creates only that which is good.

RELATIONSHIP CHALLENGES

At some time in our live we all experience difficulties concerning relationships with other people. It's a very necessary part of your life's journey. You will have had relationship difficulties that you've managed to solve easily and some that have lasted a long time, possibly years.

There will also be relationship challenges that haven't been solved before a person passed away. It's far better to solve these before the person passes away, otherwise you can be left feeling guilty.

Whatever caused your relationship challenge, there are often more than two people involved and at some time there have been angry words spoken, accusations made and nobody will give way because everyone thinks that they are right and the others are wrong.

Be prepared to discover that nobody was right, not even you. Know that the solution lies within your Spiritual Source and that is the only place where you'll find it. Prepare yourself by writing down what the challenge is. As you write it down, try not to apportion blame to any party, including yourself, just write how the situation is at this moment.

You have to let go of any preconceived ideas or solutions you may have, release your determination to be the one who is right and agree to *allow* yourself to receive the solution.

Then, and only then, do you connect to your Spiritual Source. You don't need to have your eyes closed, just find a quiet spot where you won't be disturbed. Once you've connected ask for a solution. Have a pen and pad so that you can write down whatever comes into your mind. Don't try and rationalise what you are writing, don't dispute in your mind what you are writing. Don't allow yourself to lose your feeling of peace of mind, just *allow* the words to flow.

You may find it difficult to let go the first time you try this and you may find that you've lost your peace of mind and become disconnected. Don't worry if this happens and don't feel that you have in any way failed. Just be content to try again later. This is a completely new way for you to find solutions to challenges.

You can try saying before connecting, *'I am choosing to receive the solution to this challenge'.*

There is an old proverb, *'if at first you don't succeed, try, try and try again'.* Be sure that you don't make it hard work. The secret is to feel relaxed and believe it will work for you and allow it to happen. Let go of any resistance you have – *the Law of Attraction works for everyone.*

When you have written down everything that is coming to you, read through what you've written.

You may find that you have written down something that you should do. You may find that you have to be patient and wait a little longer for the time to be right before you do anything. You may find that you need to change your attitude or viewpoint.

Whatever you have written, accept that this will be the solution or at least a starting point. If you receive a starting point and carry it through, you will begin to attract further steps to take within a very short while. It's important to be alert to receiving these further steps. You may also notice a change beginning to take place within the relationship.

You can return to your Spiritual Source at any time to discover the next solution or step to take.

If your situation concerns someone who has passed, there is still a solution. In the same way that your thoughts can be received by your Spiritual Source and your Guide, they can also be received by your loved ones who are now in the Spirit World. Before you connect, make sure that you release any feelings of guilt so that once connected you can allow the solution to flow to you.

Finding an answer to any relationship challenge will always give you a feeling of achievement, relief and peace within yourself as you realise that you have the ability to *let go* of any past concerns.

~ ~ ~ ~ ~ ~

FINANCIAL CHALLENGES

If you have financial difficulties, you need to follow the same procedure of writing down your challenge, making it very clear what you want, before making your connection.

In other words, if your challenge is lack of money, inability to pay debts, a belief that you're always going to have to struggle or that you are always going to be poor, make sure you don't worry or take those thoughts into your Connection. If you think of lack while you are 'connected', you will only attract to yourself more lack rather than the abundance which you are seeking.

Don't attempt to decide where the money is going to come from or how you are going to earn it. Let go of any thought such as 'I don't deserve it or money only comes to people who are lucky'.

As with all things, money is an energy and we create it through thought and desire. We have already created the money we are asking for. It is laid up, vibrationally speaking, in our own 'holding bay' so to speak, and when we are ready to receive it, then it will actually come to us.

You have to let go of any *resistance* to money coming to you and *allow* it to flow towards you. You'll find that money will begin to come to you in very unexpected ways. The speed at which the money flows to you is dependant on your belief that it's on its way and whether you have let go of any *resistance* that is preventing its arrival. You must *allow* the money to flow to you.

As with the solutions to relationship challenges, before connecting, write down what you want and believe that you will receive it. After you connect to your Spiritual Source write down whatever comes to you without questioning it. When you finish writing, read through what you have written and if you have received a first step, make sure that you carry it through.

Believe, expect, anticipate its arrival and you'll receive it in the right amount and at exactly the right time. Sometimes it will arrive from a totally unexpected source, such as a gift and sometimes it will arrive as a job you can do to earn the money.

If it comes as a gift you have, in some way, already earned it and it has been waiting for you to allow it to flow to you.

~ ~ ~ ~ ~ ~

HEALTH CHALLENGES

When you took on your earthly incarnation it was not your intention to have a journey of ill health. It was your intention to enjoy your journey and learn from your various experiences. It was your intention to enjoy good health.

As mentioned previously, the more you think about an illness, the more of the same you attract to yourself. Your thoughts should be focused on achieving good health. Every cell in your body has the ability to work towards keeping you healthy. Every cell knows what its job is and scientists tell us that every cell in our body has a way of communicating with every other cell.

Sometimes, we may be aware of how or why we have attracted a specific illness and at other times, we have no idea why we are suffering from ill health. Let go of the 'how' and 'why' and start to focus on creating good health.

The first step is to appreciate the health you have, the things you *are* able to do rather than focus on any present restrictions.

Before you connect to your Spiritual Source, write down the improvements you want to see to your health. When you have connected, focus all your thoughts on feeling healthy, full of energy and the ability to live your life without limitations.

Your Spiritual Source knows the solutions to all your health challenges and wants you to enjoy complete Wellbeing.

When connected, write down the solutions that flow into your mind and don't question them as you write. When you've finished, read what you've written and once again, there will be a first step to follow.

If you can only think in a positive way and *believe* that your body is responding to your positive thoughts, your health will steadily improve.

~ ~ ~ ~ ~ ~

MULTIPLE PROBLEMS

It's most likely that you have more than one challenge in your life at the moment. You may have one in each group or more than one in a particular group.

As this is a new way of living and learning from your earthly challenges it's best, at the beginning, to focus on the most important one first. In other words, as you are learning to 'connect' and reach for solutions, select the most urgent challenge first.

You'll probably find that as you allow the solutions to flow to you, more than one challenge will be solved. This is why you should confine your solution seeking to one thing at a time, because it *allows* the answer to flow to you more directly.

~ ~ ~ ~ ~ ~

WHAT TO DO NEXT

It's important that you do not under any circumstances, continue to think of your difficulties and, especially don't talk to other people about them! Focus all your thinking and talking on the *solutions* you are finding.

The big mistake that most people make is to go through the process and then think "I don't suppose it will work for me!" Remember, the Law of Attraction works for *everyone* and that includes you!

Once you have tested this process and found that it works you can use this method to solve any challenges that occur in your life. How will that feel? You have uncovered a secret that you can use at any time and in any place. The only cost is some of your time. It will be time well spent and will certainly assist you in creating the life you really want to live.

Another way is to do the following:

Before you go to sleep, spend a few moments appreciating and being grateful for everything you've received during the day. Every time you show appreciation and gratitude you become connected to your Spiritual Source.

If you make your thoughts of appreciation the last thoughts before you fall asleep, you can expect a solution to be brought to you. When you fall asleep in a place of connection, you are still connected when you wake.

As soon as you wake, write down whatever comes into your mind.

Always give thanks for the help you are receiving, whether you are receiving it directly or from a third party.

PART V

MANIFESTING YOUR DESIRES

"Do you know what you want? Are you enjoying the evolution of your desire? If you are among the rare humans who answered, "Yes, I'm enjoying the evolution of my desire," then you understand who you are and what this physical life experience is really all about."

'Abraham'

MANIFESTING YOUR DESIRES

You are a Creator and can use this to manifest your desires.

The methods you're using to solve the challenges in your life can also be used to manifest your desires. Be confident that it will work and put aside any thoughts you may have of not having whatever it is that you are desiring. Negative thoughts take away the creative power of your intention.

Before you can start to manifest your desires, you must know what you want. This may sound common sense but so many people don't know what they want. As soon as you know what you are wanting, be assured that it's on its way and begin to imagine yourself having it at all times, whether you are connected or not.

You can test whether this works by manifesting something small first. For example, some people use this for finding car parking spaces. I have been using this method for a long while and on the odd occasions when it doesn't work I've found that there is always a reason! If I cannot find a space where I want it and have to park elsewhere I either suddenly meet someone I *should* meet or pass a shop that has something in the window that I have been trying to find. This is how it works and it's amazing!

For example, if you're wanting curtains you first have to know the size of the curtains and decide on the type of curtain and the colour. Once you know exactly what you want and how much you can afford, state your intention and the Universe will hear you! This can be worded in different ways but make sure that you always use *positive* words such as:

"I desire a pair of curtains (give the size and colour) to cost no more than (the amount you've decided). I know that they are on their way and I really *appreciate* that."

Find a suitable sized box and label it My Manifesting Box. When you've decided to manifest something, write it down on a slip of paper or card and place it into your box. As you do this say

'as I place my request into my box I know it's on its way'!

When you are connected to your Spiritual Source you can imagine the curtains that are coming to you. Visualise them and how they will look at your windows and the improvement they'll make to your room.

You can use this method to manifest everything that you desire. Just begin with small things to start with, before looking for the bigger things!

You may want a new car but you have no definite idea which car, its size, colour, whether petrol or diesel, manual or automatic. As soon as you decide you want one, make sure that you have a clear picture of all the details for the car. This is really important. At the present time, you may be driving a car that is letting you down and you're feeling anxious when driving it and wondering whether you'll reach your destination.

Stop your anxious feeling and begin to feel *appreciation* for the fact that you *have* a car! When you get into your car, say to yourself that you are choosing safety for your journey and that you'll reach your destination at the correct time. Remember to send out thanks when you arrive for your safe journey. *Appreciation* is the key to everything!

Write down the details of the car you've chosen and place it into your box. Don't worry if you don't have the funds to purchase the car, just know that a way will be found for you to have the car of your dreams.

When you're connected to your Spiritual Source think of the new car that's on its way to you. Imagine how the car looks and then feel what it will be like to get into the car, how you will feel when you're driving and your pleasure in receiving it and knowing it's yours!.

Be confident that it's on its way and don't think of how it's going to manifest. It will, as long as you stay focussed and positive.

When your car arrives remember to show appreciation – this is very important.

The same thing applies if you're wanting to move home. Make a complete list of everything that you want in your new home. You have to know exactly what your new home must have and where it must be situated.

Too many people decide to move without deciding first of all exactly what they want in their new home. They find a new property and move in and very soon after they discover that there is something important missing that they should have thought of or the situation of the property is not where they want to be.

Before deciding to move begin to appreciate where you are already and look for the good points about your current home. This can make a difference to how you feel about your home and also help you to decide what you really want.

Write down exactly what you want and know that it's on it's way to you as you place it into your box.

The above examples are material items and what you are desiring may not come under this category. Whatever you want can be dealt with in the same way, written down and placed in your box.

You may be divorced and are wanting to find a new partner. Are you clear about the qualities you're looking for in a new partner and do those qualities match up with your own. It's so important to realise that you cannot change anyone but yourself.

Write down the details of the person you are wanting and place them into your box and know they'll be drawn towards you.

There is a Way

You may be considering getting divorced. Before doing so have you looked at the good qualities that your husband or wife has or only looked at the things you don't like about them?

You may be needing a certain amount of money to pay a bill that's due. You've been worrying about this and even more bills have arrived. Because you've been worrying about your lack of money to pay your bills you've attracted the same lack.

Decide how much money you need to cover your outstanding bills, write it down and place it in your box being quite certain that you are attracting it. Don't start worrying about where it's coming from as this will negate your positive statement that's in your box.

Also remember the money can come in instalments rather than in one amount and it really is on its way. If a smaller amount comes be grateful and give thanks for it. It could even be a small coin you find on the pavement. Whatever you do, don't complain that it's not enough or you will stop the next instalment arriving. However small the first amount be grateful for it and believe that more is on its way.

When you're connected to your Spiritual Source start to feel the happiness and joy of receiving.

Make it a practice to look only for solutions when you are connected to your Spiritual Source. If you consider the challenge you're facing you won't find the solution.

Have fun with your manifesting. Think of your box as a magical box which is always playing your tune and attracting to you whatever you have placed in it.

PART VI

QUESTIONS & ANSWERS

On

RELATIONSHIP CHALLENGES
FINANCIAL CHALLENGES
HEALTH CHALLENGES

"You must be the change you want to see in the world."

Mahatma Gandhi

RELATIONSHIP QUESTIONS & ANSWERS

I listened to a friend telling me about a problem she was having with a mutual friend of ours. I took her side. This caused an even bigger problem and more people became involved in the argument. What should I have done?

It's important to remember that there are always two sides to every disagreement. If you hear only one side of the story you cannot be certain that it's completely accurate. It may also be that one of the people involved has misunderstood what the other person has said.

In this type of situation it's better not to take sides but to point out the good qualities of both parties and the many happy times you have spent together in the past. It may be possible for your friend to make contact either by phone or a letter saying how she misses the friend.

Then the problem has been dealt with by her and her friend then has the choice to respond or not. If she chooses not to respond your friend has done what she can and should then be able to let go of the problem and carry on with her life.

It's important not to keep reliving it and talking about it as in time this will attract similar situations to your friend.

******

I was brought up in a loving family with very narrow religious beliefs which I was expected to follow. As I became an adult I realised that for me these beliefs were not enough. I decided to think for myself and look for answers to the many questions I had about life. This has caused family arguments every time we meet. What can I do?

First of all remember that you are not able to change anyone but yourself.

You have to be prepared to allow your family to live in the manner of their beliefs as this is their choice. You have to live according to your beliefs as this is your choice.

The suggestion here is that next time you meet, you try to avoid any confrontation. When and if the topic of beliefs crops up don't enter into an argument with them. Listen to what they have to say and allow them to have their views.

Tell them that they may be right, allow them to keep their beliefs, explain that at the present time you have chosen to have different beliefs and that you are searching for your truths.

Find something about them or their home to compliment and try to return the conversation to a more general subject. This will usually lift the atmosphere and lead to a more harmonious visit for everyone.

You can do the same thing during a telephone conversation and when you finish the call you will feel so much better.

******

I have a sibling who is jealous of me because I have a successful life and he is fed up with his life. It seems that whatever he tries to do it doesn't work. How can I help him?

If your sibling is suffering from jealousy then he will be very unhappy as jealousy always causes unhappiness.

Try to find something about him that you can compliment. Ask him what he would really like to do if he had no restrictions. Ask him what he would like his life to be like and dependant on his answers suggest that he has all the ability to succeed. Explain to him about the Law of Attraction or give him a copy of this book to read.

If he doesn't respond that's his choice and if he does respond you will have helped him to begin to change his life for the better.

If he has been jealous of you since childhood try to find out what caused this. Try to understand his thinking and tell him that you love him and only want the best for him. Just show him that you care about him and that he is very important to you.

* * * * * *

I have children who are very difficult. They have no respect for anyone including me. They are old enough to help in the home but won't and think they don't need to. How can I get them to help and show respect?

All children of every age thrive on praise. The more criticism they receive the more difficult they become. Always look for the good things about each of them and tell them how much you love them. Gradually this builds up their own self confidence and respect for themselves.

Once they respect themselves they will begin to respect others. Point out the good things about other people rather than the bad points. Always remember that nobody is perfect including you.

If they do something to help in the home remember to thank them and point out the good job they have made of it. If you want them to help ask them quietly and kindly and if they don't respond the first time just leave it. Don't make an issue of it.

Ask them in the same way again when you want their help and gradually they will begin to help more. Their respect for themselves, you and the rest of the people in the household will grow and once this happens they will begin to respect all people whoever they may be.

This may be a lengthy process but you'll find that it's been worth it in the end.

******

I am lonely. I have been looking for a partner for some years but everyone I've met doesn't seem to match my ideal person. I don't want to be on my own, how can I find the right person?

There is a Way

First of all you have to know what you are really wanting and why you are wanting that special person. You may have a list of qualities that you want to find in that person but you have to remember always that no person is perfect. You also have to admit that you are not perfect yourself.

Like attracts like and if you are looking for a person with certain qualities you have to possess those qualities yourself in order to attract them.

You also have to be content and happy with the person you are and not be looking for someone who you can totally depend on, or someone through whom you can live your life or who will live your life for you. The only person you can truly depend on is yourself and the only person who can live your life is you.

~ ~ ~ ~ ~ ~

FINANCIAL QUESTIONS & ANSWERS

I have a growing family and the costs are going up all the time but my income is not increasing at the same pace. I want to do the best for my family. I'm constantly worried about where the money will come from to pay the next bill. What can I do about this?

This is a very common problem which is experienced by many families at the present time. If like attracts like then this is what you're attracting – more money worries. In other words, you are attracting more of what you don't want. Try to stop worrying about where the money will come from and change your thoughts to finding a way to *allow* the money you need to come to you.

Spend a little while working out how much money you need each month in order to pay the family outgoings.

There is a Way

Connect with your Spiritual Source and then ask for the solution. Remember to write down whatever comes to you without questioning. It's very important to take this first step. Once you've taken this step, you will be ready to receive the next step.

If you find this difficult, use the method of 'connecting' just before you go to sleep and ask that the solution will be given to you to help you attract the sum of money you want. When you wake, immediately write down the first thing that comes into your mind. This is so often exactly the thing you need to do.

The most important thing is to stop worrying about the lack of money and put all your thoughts into finding the solution of how to attract the required money.

As long as your thoughts remain on attracting money you'll receive it, very often from a totally unexpected source.

******

I was born into a poor family where there was never any spare money for any luxuries. I decided that when I grew up I would have plenty of money. I have worked hard and built a successful business and have a wonderful wife and family and we live very comfortably. However I sense that some of my childhood friends and my birth family think I must have done something illegal to be in my present position. I'm sure it's a form of jealousy. How can I deal with this?

This problem is not really your problem. This problem belongs to the people who are jealous of your life style.

You may have at some time been with someone from your childhood who appears not to have managed to achieve what they consider a successful lifestyle. It is possible that they look at your success and feel they are unable to achieve the same.

In terms of the Law of Attraction, the more you think about such people and their attitude towards you, the more jealous people you'll meet. They may have a similar jealous nature which you recognise. In other words you have attracted these people into your life.

The way of solving this will be to look for the good things about them and if possible mention them when you're with them. This will help them to look at their own lives in a different way and gradually begin to appreciate what they have rather than what is missing.

Encouraging someone who has a problem, whether it's to do with you or not, helps to lift both your vibrations and you will no longer have to worry about people being jealous of your life.

******

I earn a reasonable salary but I overspend on luxuries that I cannot afford. I do this when I am feeling fed up seeing other people enjoying these luxury items. As a result I get behind

with my essential bills and fall into debt. How can I stop doing this?

The first step to take is to make a note of the amount of money that is coming in and add up the essential bills that have to be made each month. You will then know how much money is left for you to spend on other things. Remember that apart from the essential bills you also need money for your every day living expenses.

Once you have done this reward yourself with a small luxury item for having taken the first step to changing your life.

Worry about paying essential bills and being in debt will attract more of these worries so the next step is to put aside the money you need for your bills and/or debt payments and then you can stop worrying about them. You know that you will be able to pay them on time. Put to one side the money you will need to live and then you will be able to choose how to use what's left.

Decide what you really want to spend this money on. The luxuries that you want may be totally different to the luxuries your friends and colleagues enjoy. What is a luxury to one person is not a luxury to someone else. Within your budget, just buy what makes you happy!

Another step is to ask yourself whether there are other areas in your life that are also causing you to feel fed up. Look in the mirror and ask, "Do I value myself?" because we all overspend when we don't value ourselves.

If you want to feel good you can attract feeling good by beginning to appreciate all the good things in your life, especially life itself. As you connect with your Spiritual Source you'll discover more solutions to help you to feel good and as a result your life will begin to change in more ways than one.

******

I was brought up to believe that money was evil and therefore rich people must be evil as they all had too much money. I was taught that if rich people shared their money out then everyone would have enough. Part of me still thinks rich people must be evil but part of me knows that isn't the answer. What should I believe?

There are many very good, caring people in the world, both rich and poor. The vast majority of people who are rich use their resources in ways which help poorer people. Because one person is rich it doesn't mean that there is any less for other people.

We live in an abundant Universe where there is plenty for everyone. It is the ability to attract money and how you use it which is the important factor.

Remember that most of the rich people in the world contribute by employing people so ensuring that these people are able to earn their living. Rich people have usually worked hard to build up businesses from which other people benefit as well as themselves. Money is a unit of exchange – it is not evil. It is how we use money that's important. All things are made of energy and money is no exception.

Many rich people have set up charities or support them to help other people, either in their own countries or third world countries.

If you won the lottery and became rich, would you believe that you were now evil. Of course not! You would be the same person you were the day before but your lifestyle would probably change.

******

I am no good with money. If I have money in my pocket I spend it. Often I do this when I know the money is needed for something else such as paying the mortgage. How can I stop doing this?

The answer to this is only to carry in your pocket the money you can afford to spend. The more you think of yourself as not being any good with money the more this will be true. Your thoughts about yourself become your beliefs. They are very important.

Now is the time to let go of your belief about money and decide to change it. Look at the money you need for your mortgage and other monthly bills and set this money aside. Once you have done this you'll know how much money you have left to spend. Set a portion of this amount aside so that if something unexpected crops up you'll have some money put by that you can use.

Once you have decided that you are now going to improve your attitude about money, you'll find that more money comes in and your money will go further. There may be something you really want to buy at the moment but you don't have sufficient funds. Once you have changed your ideas and become more efficient with money, you'll find a way of buying what you want.

Believing in yourself and making practical changes which will improve your situation will also increase your general confidence.

~ ~ ~ ~ ~ ~

HEALTH QUESTIONS & ANSWERS

Wherever I go I seem to catch every virus that is around. I only have to be in a room with someone who has a cold and I know that in three days' time I'll have it. How can I avoid this?

You are attracting these illnesses because you have a belief that you are going to get them. Because you have this belief you are more aware of the people you meet who are suffering from colds and coughs. You are, in other words, attracting what you are *thinking* about.

When you can think about being well and healthy you won't notice the person in the room who has a cold and you won't then expect to catch it.

Say to yourself that you are healthy and fit and *believe* it. When you are well, you feel good and feeling good is what you are aiming for. Appreciate what's in your life now, think about how you want it to be in the future and you'll find that you will be able to attract what you want. Positive focus attracts positive results whereas negative focus attracts negative results.

The more you can connect with your Spiritual Source the better you'll feel. This will also help you to become more confident as a person and this will result in better health.

If you find yourself standing next to someone in a queue at the supermarket who is sneezing, mentally say to yourself, "I feel really well today" and then put your attention onto something else. Then release the thought of the cold from your mind and carry on with your day.

Often there is an underlying reason for becoming ill. It may be that you are unhappy with your life and need to make changes. Look into this, find the courage to makes those changes and as you begin to enjoy your life again, your health will improve.

******

As children my sister and I were very healthy. As soon as we became adults we both began to suffer continuously with one illness after another. This has caused a blight on both of our lives. We are now in our 50s and spend a lot of time in hospital. We have grown to expect that we will be ill. How can we overcome this as it also affects the lives of our families?

If you expect to be ill then you will be. Remember 'like attracts like' and because you expect to be ill that is what you attract.

When one person in a family is ill everyone within the family circle is affected in some way. If you and your sister can begin connecting to your Spiritual Sources, and start listening to what you are receiving, an improvement will be felt.

Begin by deciding that from now on you are going to start to attract better health. Because you have had so many years of health problems it may take a while for big improvements to be felt. However, recognise each small improvement and gradually you'll both begin to find good changes occurring.

Stop talking about illness and only talk about the solutions you are finding and the improvements you are feeling. This will also increase the improvements as you will be attracting that rather than further illness.

* * * * * *

My Doctor seems to be fed up with me. He says he cannot find anything wrong with me but I visit him very regularly. I just feel ill most of the time. I have had all the tests there are but nothing shows up. My Doctor told me to go away and start living. How can I do this when I constantly feel so ill?

The answer to your question is similar to the previous question. Because you are constantly thinking about how ill you feel you are attracting more of the same.

The suggestion here is that you look briefly at your life as it is and then you begin to look at the life you *really want* to lead. Earlier in this book it was suggested that you write down how you want your life to unfold from now. As you do this, don't stop and try and work out how it will happen, just write exactly what you *want.* You can always add more to it later – just make a *start*!

Once you have done this make your 'connection' with your Spiritual Source and ask for *the way forward* so your life can begin to unfold as you want. While connected, focus only on positive thoughts and then your answers will come.

Follow through with any ideas that come to you. Be positive that you are going to attract what you want and as you do this so your health will improve. It has to!

ILL HEALTH IS ONLY A TEMPORARY INDICATOR OF NEGATIVE THINKING. CHANGE YOUR THOUGHTS AND YOUR BODY WILL CHANGE, TOO. THIS IS THE LAW.

******

Three years' ago my husband left me and ever since, I have been ill. I have had one illness after another and been in hospital every time. When I'm ill my sister contacts my husband and he always comes to visit me. I look forward to his visits. Why am I always being ill and how can I avoid it?

You are attracting what you want to attract. You are 'always being ill' because you are wanting your husband to love you. You are wanting his attention and becoming ill is one way of getting it.

When you truly *want* to be *well* and happy, your body (which is listening to you) will begin to improve. Your body's natural state is to be well, but when we are upset emotionally, that negativity prevents the body from working properly.

Begin to *accept* and love yourself because the truth is to be truly happy, you need you more than your husband.

You are obviously unhappy about your husband leaving and your unhappiness has attracted ill health. Because when you are ill your husband visits, you are attracting further illnesses so that he will visit again. This is quite a common problem.

As with the answer to the previous question you now have a choice. Decide what you *want.* You obviously don't want to keep suffering from ill health, therefore choose to feel good. It is when you feel good that you can enjoy your life. So start *NOW*!

Start by *appreciating* what you have rather than complaining about what is missing. Connect with your Spiritual Source for the solutions you need. If, for example, you don't *know* how you want your life to be, when you are connected, ask for help in finding the first step. It may be a very small step but that doesn't matter. Once you make a start you'll find it will become easier with each step you take.

******

I have an elderly Mother who has poor health. She lives alone and is always phoning for me to come quickly as she thinks she may be dying. By the time I arrive she is feeling better. Is this her way of controlling my life. Does she know she is doing this and how can I stop her?

Much like the previous question, your Mother is using her fear of dying to get your attention and she is succeeding!

She is probably lonely and may be frightened of being on her own. She may or may not be aware of what she is doing to you but she needs help and so do you.

If she could have someone visit other than yourself this could help. Often an elderly person is completely different with someone outside the family than when a close family person is with them. If it's possible to have a word with her Doctor you should be able to find out whether her health is contributing to how she is behaving.

You will know your Mother better than anyone. In your earlier life was she a controlling person? Was she always telling you what to do or demanding attention? Is she behaving suddenly in a way you wouldn't expect her to behave? The answer to these questions may be helpful to the Doctor.

If you can connect with your Spiritual Source, asking only for guidance, you will be given the direction to take. Remember it's your Mother's problem and you cannot make her change but you can alter the way *you* look at the problem.

I would also suggest that you send out healing thoughts for her, asking that she receives whatever she needs.

You will find that by connecting to your Spiritual Source you'll receive the strength that *you* need to cope with the situation and your Mother will in turn, receive what *she* needs.

"Every moment that my thought feels good, I am fueling my wellness."

'Abraham'

PART VII

CONCLUSION

TO LIVE NOT EXIST

"As you continue to send out love, the energy returns to you in a regenerating spiral. As love accumulates, it keeps your system in balance and harmony. Love is the tool, and more love is the end product."

Sara Paddison

As you reach the end of this book ask yourself the following questions:

- ***Am I experiencing more joy and happiness on my life's journey?***

- ***How do I now feel after reading this book?***

- ***Do I want to test this process for myself?***

- ***Do I know what I want for my journey?***

- ***Am I going to start working towards what I want?***

- ***Am I able to change my thinking patterns?***

- ***Is my life improving as I change my thoughts?***

- ***Am I beginning to attract what I want?***

- ***Am I seeking solutions rather than focusing on problems?***

Be really honest with yourself as you answer the above questions. Every question should be answered with **yes!**

You can read this book as many times as you like but it's only by testing it for yourself that you will know for certain that the processes really do work. You may have found the book interesting to read but the real proof lies in you testing it and discovering that it is helping you to work through all challenges.

You will always encounter challenges on your life's journey and to know you have the resources and the spiritual 'tools' within you, to face each and every situation, will make the journey much easier. You have it within you to create a life of adventure, love, happiness and joy. It's up to you! Good luck!

MAY YOU HAVE EVERY SUCCESS WITH YOUR LIFE'S JOURNEY, MAY YOU ALWAYS BE CONNECTED TO YOUR SPIRITUAL SOURCE, MAY YOU LIVE JOYFULLY, MAY YOU FULFIL YOUR PURPOSE AND MANIFEST YOUR DREAMS, MAY YOU LOVE AND BE LOVED.

BECAUSE

THIS IS YOUR NEW BEGINNING. LIFE DOES NOT END. LIFE IS ETERNAL

SD - #0015 - 070726 - C0 - 210/148/8 - PB - 9781780350035 - Gloss Lamination